**Essential Quest...**
Why do people immigrate to new places?

# Gustaf
## Goes to America

★ ★ ★ ★ ★ ★ ★ ★ ★ ★ ★ ★ ★

by rica Larssen · illustrated by Eric Scott Fisher

# CHAPTER 1

★ ★ ★ ★ ★

# Tales of America

"Tell me some more about America," I begged my Uncle Lars.

"It's the land of plenty, Gustaf," he said.

"Is that why you have so much money to spend?" I asked jokingly. Uncle Lars had brought us all presents when he came to visit our village. He had arrived two weeks ago, and since that time all he talked about was America. I couldn't get enough of his tales. Now he was going back, working on a cargo ship carrying a load of iron to New York. I was waiting at the station with him, eager for every last scrap of information.

"There's money to be made, that's for sure," he said. "They're giving away good land, too. You just need to agree to work it for five years."

"I'm a hard worker, Uncle. Take me with you, and I'll get myself a farm."

"I'm sorry, Gustaf, but you are too valuable to your family here," he said. I could tell he felt sorry about it. He knew I did not like working for Farmer Muller.

"Did you know that your old friend Jim Swenson was here last month, Uncle?" I asked. "He lives in Chicago now. The city is growing, and he earns ten times as much as he did in Sweden. His suit was made of wool so fine that Rosie thought he must be a millionaire."

"Your sister has always had an eye for clothes," my uncle said. "Now, tell me what other news you heard from Jim Swenson."

"He was shocked by the price of food in the village market, and we told him how bad our harvests were this year. He said food was cheap in America."

As I watched my uncle board his train, I wanted to jump on with him. I thought about stowing away on his ship and then, if I was caught, diving overboard and swimming to America.

But instead I waved good-bye to Uncle Lars and trudged back home. I knew my youngest brother Olaf would be waiting for me, eager to spin a tall tale about wild animals with eyes like fire and teeth like swords.

And so he was. "You just missed a very big wolf," he said. "I chased him off."

I tried to smile at Olaf as he opened the gate for me, but the smile wouldn't come.

After my uncle's visit, winter settled like a heavy blanket over the village. Winters in Sweden are long and dark. In the evenings, we all made things to sell at the market. My father and my brother Michael made furniture out in the cold barn. I was lucky. I got to sit by the fire with my sister and young Olaf. My sister knitted caps, shawls, and scarves. Olaf helped out and entertained us with his stories. Meanwhile, Mother made butter and cheese using the milk from our two cows.

# CHAPTER 2

★ ★ ★ ★ ★

# A Difficult Decision

It was a very hard winter. One evening, I sat with Mother, Father, Michael, Rosie, and Olaf. The fire crackled, knives scraped on wood, and knitting needles clicked. My mother cleared her throat.

"Children, your father and I have something to tell you. We sold the two cows."

"But Mother," said Rosie. "Sadie and Ella were part of the family."

Everybody was sad to hear the news.

"We had no choice," said Father. "There are six mouths to feed, and we needed money."

"I think it was a good idea," said Michael. "I am sick of eating potato soup for every meal."

I looked at the faces of my family and thought about my uncle and Jim Swenson, who both returned from America well-fed and cheerful, with money in their pockets. "In this country there are too many people, there isn't enough land, and the crops are failing," I said.

"Thank you, Gustaf, for stating our troubles so plainly," said my father.

"In America," I said, "there is good land just waiting for someone to farm it."

"I suppose the streets are paved with gold, too," said my father.

"No, but in summer the fields are full of golden wheat, as far as the eye can see," I said.

Rosie looked at me sharply. "We need you here," she said.

"It will be better for all of us if I try my luck in America," I said. "I will send money back, and it will soon be more than I earn working for Farmer Muller."

My mother sighed, and I knew that if she told me to stay, I would stay.

To my surprise, she said, "You are 18, Gustaf. You know your own mind. Try your luck in America, but keep us in your thoughts."

One morning in early February, I got up before dawn. It was time to go. My mother had been saving some bread and sliced sausage. She gave it to me to eat on my journey.

Everyone said good-bye as though they would never see me again. My mother hugged me. My brother Michael shook my hand. My sister Rosie cried like a baby and begged me to write. My father told me not to forget the family once I landed in America. He said that if I tried always to do the right thing, as he had taught me, all would be well. Young Olaf said nothing. He just looked at me angrily.

"I need you here to keep the family safe," I said to him, "but it won't be long before you can visit me on my farm."

Olaf nodded seriously, then tugged my arm. I bent down.

"Watch out for bears," he whispered in my ear. Then he waved me off.

# CHAPTER 3

★ ★ ★ ★ ★

# To America

It was a 20 mile walk to the railway station. I then caught a train to the port city of Gothenberg. From there, a ship would take me all the way to New York. I traveled in steerage, where I had a bed and plenty of food. Most of the people in steerage were Swedes, and there was music and dancing for those who were not seasick. I also studied English on the journey.

After seven weeks on board ship, I arrived in New York. I then made my way, by train and by wagon, to Minnesota.

At the end of the summer, I sent my first letter home to the family. I told them about my new job working for a farmer named Jonsen.

The Jonsens gave me room and board. In return, I worked on the farm. Most days I ate with the other farm workers. On Sundays I had a meal with the Jonsen family.

"How do you like American life?" said Mrs. Jonsen one Sunday. She was piling up a plate with roast chicken, gravy, boiled potatoes, and greens. The Jonsens were from Sweden like me, but they preferred to eat like Americans now.

"I like it fine," I said. Even as I spoke, I wondered if that was true. I worked from morning to night, sending money home to my family. This new life was not so different from my old life. I was impatient for the day when I had land of my own.

"Would you rather be back home? I believe the harvest was better this year, but every week there are more Swedes arriving in Minnesota," said Mr. Jonsen.

"You are right," I said. "Crops grow like weeds here, and you have wonderful machines to help with planting and harvesting. It is a good place to be a farmer."

# CHAPTER 4

★ ★ ★ ★ ★

# The First Christmas

One day, just before Christmas, I stopped by the Jonsen's house.

I was feeling a little sad. The mail had been really slow, and I had not had a letter from my family for a month. I imagined everyone at home preparing a big Christmas feast. Even when times were hard, my mother would prepare a delicious meal. Her rice pudding was my favorite.

Mrs. Jonsen smiled when she saw me. She was holding something in her hand.

"Here, Gustaf, these letters came for you. They were waiting at the general store."

I carefully inspected the two letters. The first letter was from the government, and it contained good news. I was going to be a homesteader!

I pictured a plot of land covered in trees, with a river nearby for water. The first thing to do would be to clear the trees, then cut the logs into timber to build a house.

"Don't forget the other letter," said Alice, the Jonsen's daughter. "It's from Sweden."

I eagerly ripped open the second letter, which was from my sister Rosie. She said that the family were all busy planning a huge celebration because my uncle would be home for Christmas.

Rosie continued:

I have news about Michael. As you know, he has been wanting to join you in America and Mother and Father have finally agreed that he can go next year, if there is work for him at the Jonsen's farm.

I will write again soon.

Your loving sister,

Rosie

At that moment, I felt happier than I had been in months. Michael could work for the Jonsens, and after a while I hoped he would help me clear my land. I was sure that it would not be too long before he had land of his own to work. After all, this was the land of plenty!

I felt like an excited child as I began to share the news with the Jonsens. Then, as I was passing the letters around, I saw that there were still two items in Rosie's envelope. One was a small photograph of my parents, with a message written on the back that said, "We hope to join you one day in America."

The other item was a sketch Olaf had made of our little house in the village. He had drawn himself chasing a fire-breathing dragon that was running away from the house. Under the picture he'd written a message to me. It said, "Don't worry, I'm taking care of things here."

I knew that when I built my homestead, these two pictures would take a place of pride.

## Summarize

Think about the details in *Gustaf Goes to America*. Summarize the main events in the story. The details from your Theme Chart may help you.

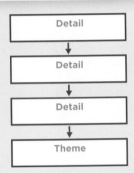

## Text Evidence

1. How do you know that *Gustaf Goes to America* is a fiction text? What kind of fiction is it? How do you know? GENRE

2. Why does Gustaf want to go to America? THEME

3. On page 5, what does Gustaf compare winter to? What did he mean? SIMILES

4. Why do you think Gustaf is telling his story? Write about the message you think Gustaf is trying to get across. Use details from the story to support your answer. WRITE ABOUT READING

**Compare Texts**

Read how Swedish Americans celebrate their culture.

# Celebrating Swedish Culture

In the 1860s, life was hard in Scandinavian countries such as Sweden and Norway. They had too many people, not enough good land, and not enough food to go around. Meanwhile, in America the government was giving land to settlers who would farm it for at least five years. Many Swedes began to see America as the land of opportunity.

Between 1860 and 1930, large numbers of Swedes decided to immigrate to the Midwestern United States. They brought their Swedish culture and traditions with them. Swedish Americans still celebrate their culture in America today.

Swedes and Norwegians in the Midwest in 1872

**Key** (people per square mile)

1–3  3–6
6–15  15+

Many Swedish Americans celebrate traditional Swedish holidays. One of these is Midsummer's Day, on the third Sunday in June. A decorated pole, called a maypole, is raised in an outdoor area. People dance and sing around the maypole. This day is celebrated as Swedish Day. It is a special festival of Swedish culture with picnics, parades, and folk dancing.

Another Swedish holiday is Saint Lucia's Day, which once marked the longest day of winter in Sweden.

Dancing and singing around a maypole is a Swedish tradition that has been brought to some parts of America.

Swedish Americans celebrate by eating food that was once eaten throughout Sweden. There is always plenty of meat, fish, potatoes, and pickled vegetables. There are also baked goods, including many types of bread, pastries, and cookies. Swedish immigrants to America introduced their adopted country to the smorgasbord. For a smorgasbord, all of the food is laid out on a table and guests can help themselves to the dishes they like.

A smorgasbord is usually served at celebrations. There is always plenty of food, including fish, such as salmon.

## Make Connections

What does *Celebrating Swedish Culture* tell you about why people from Sweden moved to the United States? ESSENTIAL QUESTION

Why do many people like to celebrate with traditional food when they immigrate to new places? Use examples from *Gustaf Goes to America* and *Celebrating Swedish Culture* to support your response. TEXT TO TEXT

## Focus on Genre

**Historical Fiction** Historical fiction tells a story that is set in the past. The settings are realistic and drawn from history and may contain historical persons, but the main characters are usually made up.

**Read and Find** *Gustaf Goes to America* tells a story that happened in the past. It describes a particular period in American history. The author researched the stories of immigrants to America and used facts from their stories in this story. For example, the details about how people traveled to America from Sweden are true.

### Your Turn

Choose a time in the past and research some facts about that time. Write a story set in the past using the facts you have researched. Have your characters do things that people in that time would have done.